Bill & Bob

A Play

H. Connolly

SAMUELFRENCH-LONDON.CO.UK
SAMUELFRENCH.COM

FOR AMATEUR PRODUCTION ENQUIRIES

UNITED KINGDOM AND WORLD EXCLUDING NORTH AMERICA
plays@SamuelFrench-London.co.uk
020 7255 4302/01

Each title is subject to availability from Samuel French,

depending upon country of performance.

CHARACTERS

Bob, late 40s
Bill, a Scotsman; early 40s
Mo (Maureen), Bob's wife; about 40
Jane, Bill's wife; 30s

The action of the play takes place in Bill's and Bob's workplace, Bob's kitchen and Bill's front room

Time — the present

Other plays by H. Connolly
published by Samuel French Ltd

Daddy's Gone A-Hunting
One Careful Owner
Overtime

For Charley

BILL & BOB

Bill's and Bob's workplace, Bob's kitchen and Bill's front room

The set is divided into three small areas. UC *is a space denoting Bill's and Bob's workplace, with two wooden chairs — one of which is wobbly — with an upturned tea chest between them which Bill and Bob use as a table.* DR *is Bob's kitchen, with a table and two chairs set on a bit of lino.* DL *is Bill's front room, in which an armchair and a small side table, upon which is a photo frame, are set on a bit of carpet. The three areas are lit independently*

When the play begins the area UC *is lit*

Bob enters wearing a long brown working jacket and carrying two mugs of tea, one very large, the other small. He also carries his lunch bag and has a newspaper under his arm. He puts the mugs on the tea chest and sits on the wobbly chair. He gets up, looks across the room to make sure nobody is coming, and swaps the chairs over. He sits again, realizes he has given himself the small mug of tea and swaps the two mugs over. He reads the paper and drinks his tea

Bill, a Scotsman, enters from the opposite side of the room. He is also wearing a long brown working jacket

Bob (*looking up from his paper*) There you are … I didn't think you
    were stopping this morning.
Bill You won't believe it, Bob. I got caught by that knob-head of
    a foreman, didn't I? Had to take the forklift down to level two and
    unload a delivery.
Bob Your tea's on the table.
Bill Ta. (*He drinks*) Why do deliveries always come at break times?
    (*He sits*)

Bob (*still reading*) I think lorry drivers are born with a sixth sense — they can hear a tea bag hit the bottom on a mug from ten miles away!

Bill That last one couldn't reverse to save his life. All over the place like measles he was.

Bob The tosser!

Bill I shouted to him: "I wouldn't let you drive sheep, mate." That's when he hit the wall.

Bob It has to be an agency driver.

Bill So, I pulls open his door to ask if he's paid for his ride on the dodgems and you'll never believe what happened next.

Bob He hit you?

Bill No — the bloke only got out and it was a woman driver, weren't it?

Bob No!

Bill Yeah, it was … A split-ass mechanic — as true as I'm sat here on this wobbly chair (*He gets up and looks at the chair*)

Bob (*putting down the paper*) Did she have big knockers?

Bill puts his hands up to show that she did

No wonder she couldn't reverse then. (*He puts the paper on the tea chest*)

Bill It's funny that, ain't it? A woman with big knockers just can't reverse. (*He rocks his chair*) My seat's wobbly.

Bob (*to himself; thoughtfully*) Must be because they can't turn their heads right round.

Bill You've swapped seats, haven't you?

Bob You can only get a woman to use a mirror for two things. Putting on their make-up and exploring themselves down below.

Bill (*still looking at the chair*) It wasn't wobbly yesterday.

Bob Good job I wasn't there.

Bill (*sitting again*) No — you'd have been dribbling from both ends, you randy old goat, you.

Bob I've always had a love for the ladies.

Bill (*wobbling the seat*) Are you sure this ain't your chair?

Bob Some men, such as yourself, have a taste for the beer. My weakness has always been for the fairer sex. For some strange reason they seem to find me attractive.
Bill Ay — very strange.

Bob looks at Bill. Bill wiggles in the chair

I'll get a screw for it after lunch.
Bob Will you stop fidgeting on that chair ... You look like a man driven mad by piles!
Bill But it's wobbly.
Bob Is it?
Bill And it wasn't yesterday. (*He puts his head between his knees and looks at the underside of his chair*)
Bob Now what you doing?
Bill (*from under the chair*) Looking for chewing gum.
Bob For God's sake! I know you're Scottish, but that's ridiculous!
Bill (*sitting up*) There was a big lump of chewing gum under my seat yesterday and now it's gone.
Bob I'll call security then, shall I? Get them to comb the whole building, room by room.
Bill I noticed yours was wobbly yesterday.
Bob Don't worry about a bloody chair. I've got a bit of news for you.
Bill You have?
Bob I've only gone and cracked that blonde secretary from level five.
Bill Never!
Bob Yes ... She gave me her mobile number this morning.
Bill But she told you to piss off when you whistled at her yesterday.
Bob Playing hard to get, weren't she?
Bill (*puzzled*) But then she slapped your face.
Bob That was just a little bit of foreplay.
Bill Bloody hell. I'd hate to see her in full throes of passion, then!
Bob I reckon she's married.
Bill Yeah, she looks miserable enough. How many have you been through in this building now?

Bob I don't like to blow my own trumpet, but when you're as smooth as I am, you don't have to.

Bill I don't know how you do it. I really don't.

Bob It's all in the chat-up lines.

Bill You've got something, Bob, I'll give you that. But it can't be anything to do with looks.

Bob What do you mean?

Bill Well, you're hardly Brad Pitt are you?

Bob I don't know.

Bill More like — coal pit, I'd say.

Bob Yes, well, it's the rugged look that attracts. No, I tell you mate, she looks a sophisticated woman, this one.

Bill She looks a stuck-up old cow to me. Anyway, if she's so sophisticated like you say, what's she doing giving you her mobile number?

Bob She can see beneath all this garb. (*He points to his jacket*) Underneath she knows I'm a man who's going places.

Bill Of course you're going places — you're a forklift driver. (*He laughs at his joke*)

Bob You can laugh, but I tell you, you've got to know how to treat a women. Keep 'em working, keep 'em guessing or keep 'em pregnant: that's my motto.

Bill What about fidelity?

Bob Who's she?

Bill No, Mo, your wife. What about her?

Bob Oh, I've still got enough energy for her at nights.

Bill What if she finds out you've been messing about with other women?

Bob How's she going to find out? No, I tell you mate, ignorance is bliss. And going by that, she's as happy as half a pig in a freezer.

Bill You've got a lot of neck, you have.

Bob I've got a lot of something, but it's nothing to do with neck!

Both men laugh out loud. Pause

Bill You've not forgotten you're covering for me tomorrow afternoon, have you?

Bob No, mate. You're all right. You're in court for slapping that boy behind the counter in McDonald's, aren't you?

Bill He upset me, Bob. He poked his tongue out at me.

Bob He was showing you his new stud.

Bill Ay, and I showed him the back of my hand.

Bob But why?

Bill Because he had a Glasgow Rangers shirt on.

Bob How do you know that?

Bill I could smell it under his coat.

Bob So that's a good enough reason to smack him, then, is it?

Bill (*banging the tea chest, then standing*) It is if you're a Celtic man!

Bob I don't believe you.

Bill It was a Saturday night, Bob.

Bob Oh, you should have said. The judge will probably let you off, then.

Bill I was drunk.

Bob It was a quarter to six in the evening!

Bill I'll have to take your word for that.

Bob What did your wife make of it?

Bill Jane? She was stood behind me in the queue.

Bob What did she say?

Bill Well, at first she sucked her breath in like a Dyson. Then she made out she was an illegal immigrant and had never seen me before in her life. (*He sits*)

Bob Tell me more, please.

Bill Then the manager came running out and he slipped on a chip and stuck his hand in the deep fat fryer.

Bob No!

Bill Ay. But not for long. And the language, Bob … !

Bob I bet!

Bill Terrible. With all those wee bairns looking on, too. I told him: "You're not setting a very good example to the wee ones."

Bob But you'd just …

Bill (*looking at Bob*) What?

Bob Nothing. So then what happened?

Bill (*standing and pointing to his groin*) He only tried to kick me in the McNuggets!

Bob No!
Bill Ay. Just because I put a splash of vinegar on his hand.

Bob looks at Bill

I thought vinegar was good for burns.
Bob But it wasn't?
Bill No. It's good for more bad language, though. (*He sits*) It was then me and the illegal immigrant decides to leg it up the road. Coincidentally, just as the manager 'phoned the police.
Bob How did the police catch you?
Bill They didn't. As we were running up the road, Jane decides she's had enough, jumps on me and makes a citizen's arrest in the middle of the street!
Bob What did the Old Bill make of that?
Bill Oh, they thought it was hilarious. They could hardly get the cuffs on me for laughing. It's so embarrassing; arrested by my own wife!
Bob You've got to give up drinking at weekends, Bill. It always gets you into trouble.
Bill But I enjoy it. It's my hobby.
Bob In the last few months you've been found asleep in a builder's skip and you've thrown up into a restaurant's fish tank.
Bill Have you seen tropical fish in a feeding frenzy?
Bob Then the other week you took the microphone off a man in a club and sang *Flower of Scotland* all night.
Bill I was doing karaoke.
Bob Yes, but everybody else was there to play bingo.
Bill *Flower of Scotland* is a fine uplifting song, don't you think?

Bob grunts and reads his paper

(*Standing*) I'd like to say something in my defence.
Bob What's that?

Bill looks at Bob, then sits

Bill No. I'd like to be able to say something, but I can't think of anything. Neither can my lawyer.

Bob What did your lawyer recommend?
Bill That my wife divorces me.
Bob I don't know how she puts up with you.
Bill She'll never leave me, that one. I'm stuck with her for life.
Bob So, are you pleading guilty?
Bill I was provoked Bob. He snatched the money off me.
Bob I can't wait to read about it in the local rag. It will be a bloody scream, I reckon. (*He picks up his paper*)
Bill (*suddenly serious*) Ay, bloody hell, I hadn't thought of that.
Bob It might even make the local news on telly. (*He reads his paper*)
Bill (*looking at Bob*) You don't really think so, do you?
Bob Oh yeah, this time tomorrow you'll be a bloody celebrity mate.

Bill looks worried. Bob looks at him

Look, don't worry. It won't affect your job here; your behaviour's always impeccable at work.
Bill Yeah. Anyway, there'll be too much real news for them to be bothered about that — (*he thinks*) hopefully!

There is the sound of a bleeper

Bob Hang on. (*He puts his hand in his pocket*) My bleeper's going. (*He takes the bleeper out of his pocket and looks at it*) I don't believe it. Another lorry's turned up at teatime.
Bill You can go this time.
Bob (*folding his paper and putting it in his pocket*) Yeah. Knowing my luck it will be Benny with the BO. (*He stands up*)

Bill grabs his chair and turns it upside down under his arm

What are you doing with that?
Bill I'm inspecting it. Ahh, there you are. (*He points to the bottom of the chair*) A blob of Juicy Fruit, if I'm not mistaken. (*He looks at Bob*) Case proven, me lord.
Bob OK. You've got me, bang to rights. You can have it back at dinnertime. (*He heads for the exit*)

Bill takes the paper from Bob's pocket, unnoticed by Bob, as Bob goes out

> *Bill swaps the chairs back over, then exits carrying the wobbly one*

The Lights cross-fade to the DR area, Bob's kitchen

> *Bob enters wearing his own jacket and carrying his lunch bag*

> *Mo enters*

Mo Oh, hallo. What are you doing home so early?
Bob Ain't I allowed to be?

Bob gives Mo his lunch bag

Mo Of course. (*She kisses him on the cheek*) Do you want your dinner now or not? It's ready.
Bob Yeah, great. I'm starving. (*He puts his jacket over the back of his chair*)

> *Mo exits into the kitchen with the bag*

(*Sitting at the table*) Bill's covering for me for a couple of hours.
Mo (*off*) That's nice of him.
Bob Yeah, mind you, I've got to do the same for him tomorrow afternoon when he goes to court.

> *Mo enters carrying a large plate of sausages and mash*

Mo What's it for this time? (*She puts the plate on the table and sits on a chair*)
Bob I told you. He hit that lad that cheeked him in McDonald's. (*He looks at her*) No sauce.
Mo I'm sorry.

> *Mo exits*

Bob I think he's really worried about it this time. So I told him I'd stand as a character witness for him if he liked.

A crash is heard in the kitchen

Are you all right?
Mo (*off*) Yes … yes, I'm fine.

Mo comes in carrying a bottle of sauce

You didn't, really, did you? (*She gives Bob the bottle*)
Bob Of course I did. (*He opens the bottle and smacks the bottom to get the sauce out*)
Mo Do you think that's a good idea? (*She sits*)
Bob What?
Mo Being a character witness for Bill … I mean, you don't really know him.
Bob (*putting the top back on the bottle*) I've worked with him for nearly three years.
Mo Yes, but you don't really know anything about him outside work.
Bob He works hard. He's reliable. He don't swear in mixed company and he reads books. (*He eats*)
Mo What's reading books got to do with anything?
Bob It's the kind of books he reads, that's what counts. (*He eats his dinner with one arm around the plate*) Not any run-of-the-mill old rubbish about war, cowboys or shagging.
Mo Bob!
Bob No, these books are big with hard covers and are all about the mind and psychology and things that a forklift driver has no business knowing about.
Mo But he's a drunk.
Bob I think he's a lot cleverer than he lets on.
Mo So, he's a clever drunk.
Bob Anyway, I felt obliged to offer, seeing as I'm his superior.
Mo You're only superior because you drive a bigger forklift.
Bob And I've been there longer than he has and I'm trusted with the keys to open up every morning.

Mo So where are the keys now?
Bob Billy's got them. He's going to lock … (*He looks at Mo*)

Mo looks away

Anyway, he didn't want my help. Said he had to sort it out for himself. (*He eats*)
Mo (*standing; nervously*) I'm not very happy that you're asking him and his wife to our Mandy's wedding.
Bob (*looking up*) Why not?
Mo I have visions of him throwing up all over the reception.
Bob Why would he do that?
Mo Why not … If what you tell me is true, his trail of vomit is legendary over six counties.
Bob All right, love. I'm trying to eat my sausage and mash here.
Mo Sorry. I just don't want anything to go wrong. God knows I'm nervous enough about it all now. (*She sits*)
Bob Trust me. You haven't even met the man. You don't know him.
Mo Yes, and that's how I'd really like to keep it.
Bob All the kids married before they were twenty. (*He thinks*) Lovely jubberley – that gives us plenty of time together to do what we want.
Mo Bob … There's something I've been meaning to ask you …
Bob I thought maybe we could get a caravan, or even a camper van would do. (*He eats and talks at the same time*) Come home from work on a Friday and hit the open road. The New Forest, the Lake District, Stonehenge. (*He thinks*) Well, maybe not Stonehenge. (*He puts a mouthful of food in*)
Mo Bob … I want another baby.

Bob splutters as his food goes down the wrong way

Are you all right? Don't panic. Try to relax.

Bob chokes harder

Bob (*croaking*) Water — water!

Mo exits into the kitchen

Bob chokes on his own

Mo enters with a glass of water

Mo Dear God! You're going blue!

Mo gives Bob the water and he drinks. She slaps his back several times, spilling water everywhere

Bob All right … All right!

Mo stops. Bob coughs and wipes his eyes with a hanky

Mo Are you OK?
Bob (*still struggling to speak*) What are you trying to do … ? Kill me?
Mo Sorry, I didn't mean to shock you. (*She sits*)
Bob Shock me … Shock me? (*He drinks again*)
Mo I've been thinking about it and it's what I really want.

Bob is still wiping his face with his hanky

Bob, are you all right?
Bob (*looking up, his mood darkening*) Are you trying to take the mickey out of me, girl?
Mo Babies are all I know, Bob.
Bob How can we have another baby? You know it's not possible. What about your age?
Mo We could always adopt.
Bob Adopt?
Mo Yes. I've been and got us some information. (*She takes a leaflet from her pocket*)
Bob God, you've put me right off my dinner. (*He pushes it away*)
Mo Are you going to finish it?
Bob No, I can't face it now.

Mo (*picking up Bob's plate*) I'll pop it in the oven. You might
 fancy it later.

Mo exits into the kitchen

Bob You're joking! I'll never be able to eat sausage and mash
without oxygen ever again! Bring us a beer from the fridge, will
you? (*To himself*) God knows I could do with one. (*He looks at
the leaflet, then throws it across the table*)

Mo enters with a can of beer which she gives to Bob

Mo Perhaps if you thought about it for a few days …
Bob I don't need to think about it. I don't want one. God knows
we've done our bit — we've brought three of our own up, haven't
we? That's more than enough for any couple, I'd have thought.
(*He opens the can and drinks*)
Mo It's all right for you. You're still at work. What about me? What
am I going to do now all the children have flown the nest?
Bob Look after me, I hope.
Mo Yes, but that's not a proper job.
Bob Get a hobby then.
Mo I don't want a hobby.
Bob But what about my caravan?
Mo We could still do that.
Bob Not if we adopt a kid we can't. (*He thinks*) What about a dog?
Mo I don't want a dog.
Bob Think about it. They're loveable, friendly, loyal ——
Mo I don't want a dog!
Bob They don't live as long as a kid.
Mo *Bob!* (*She bangs the table in frustration and walks away*)
Bob I don't want a kid. I want a caravan.
Mo We could take him with us.
Bob (*turning up his nose*) But kids are always sick everywhere.
Mo (*through gritted teeth*) We can call him Billy then, can't we?
Bob Yes but … (*He thinks*) Hang on, you said "he".
Mo Well, after three girls of your own, I thought you might like a
boy.

Bob thinks for a moment

Bob A boy? (*He snaps out of it*) Oh no … No … No … You're not getting me like that.
Mo Well, it's up to you, Bob. Either we look into adopting a little boy — or I'm going to get a proper job. (*She sits*)
Bob (*laughing*) You?
Mo Yes, why not?
Bob But you've never had a proper job.

Mo looks at him

Well, apart from bringing up three kids.
Mo And running a house, looking after the garden, supplying a taxi service, nurse, maid, handyman, moneylender, babysitter, skivvy, seamstress and washerwoman.
Bob OK — OK. I get the whole CV.
Mo Anyway, you're forgetting. I did use to work for a living once.
Bob (*looking at Mo*) But that was years ago, before we were married.
Mo I wouldn't mind going back to being a secretary.
Bob (*his mood darkening again*) You needn't think you're going to be doing that. You can get any idea of that right out of your head. (*He stands*)
Mo But why not? I know it would be difficult … I mean, it's all computers now, but I could retrain.

Bob slams the table with his fist. Mo jumps

Bob (*getting angry*) I know what you're trying to do. I've sussed out your little game.
Mo What game?
Bob Adopting a baby's just a ploy to get what you really want. You think I'd be so shocked about the whole idea, that I'd be only too happy to let you get dressed up to the nines and go and be some randy bastard's secretary!
Mo Bob!
Bob Well, I guess I couldn't blame you, really.

Mo That's not what I want at all.

Bob Do you think I don't know what goes on behind the closed doors? All the laughing and joking — the groping and fondling. The long lunches and the business trips with the boss!

Mo Bob! Please.

Bob I've seen it with my own eyes over the last five years. Slappers, the lot of them!

Mo Don't talk to me like that, Bob. I'm your wife!

Bob turns away from Mo

I only want a life, Bob. (*She moves to him*) Just like everyone else.

Bob (*not looking at her*) You have got a life. This house …

Mo Can't you see? It's become my prison.

They stand for a few moments back to back; then Bob grabs his jacket

Where are you going?

Bob To the pub.

Mo What about your dinner?

Bob Stuff it! (*He puts on his jacket*)

Mo We really need to talk about this.

Bob (*putting his finger to Mo's face*) There's nothing to talk about. I've made my mind up so that's an end to all this silly chatter. Don't wait up. I'm going to be late.

Bob exits

Mo (*shouting after him*) But you've not had anything to eat. (*She sits*) Oh Bob … Bob. Why do you always shut me out?

The Lights cross-fade to Bill's front room DL

Bill enters, takes off his jacket, sits in the armchair, sighs, rubs his eyes, and then removes his tie

The front door slams shut, off stage

Bill (*sinking further into the chair*) Oh my God!

Jane screams, off. Something smashes against a wall

Jane storms in

Jane That has to be the most embarrassing experience of my whole life!
Bill (*not looking at her*) It wasn't that bad.
Jane Ha … Not that bad, he says … Not that bad. Our good name has been dragged through the gutter. I won't be able to walk down the High Street ever again without people pointing and laughing at me behind my back. And as for going into the local shop … ? Well, you can forget that!
Bill People will forget in time.
Jane I won't. The shame will live with me forever. I might as well have it tattooed on my forehead.
Bill Don't over-dramatize things.
Jane Over-dramatize? (*She moves to him*) Do you know I've never even been into a courtroom until today? Just how much further down do you think this ridiculous situation can drag us? How much longer before it robs us of everything?
Bill It was just a one-off. It's never ended up in court before.
Jane It's never involved violence before, either. (*She kneels before Bill*) Don't you see? It's getting worse month by month, little by little. (*She grabs his arm*) You're supposed to be a clever man, Billy. Even you must see, you can't control this now.
Bill It's all right. I'll make it better for both of us.
Jane You've got to do more than that, Billy. (*She stands*) Do you remember what we talked about on my birthday?

Bill looks at Jane, then looks away

I want you to promise me again you'll do what we agreed.
Bill (*standing; very slightly angry*) We didn't talk about it and it most definitely wasn't agreed!
Jane (*shouting*) You promised! You promised, you bastard, you know you did! (*She lashes out at Bill*)

Bill (*grabbing Jane's arms to protect himself*) I never.

Pause

Jane You would do it if you loved me.
Bill You can't doubt how I feel for you.

Pause

Jane (*turning away from him*) You're weak. You've always been weak. You talk the big talk, but when it really comes to it, you're a pathetic, weak, little bastard.
Bill Stop it woman! For God's sake, haven't we been through enough today?

Jane stands in silence for a while

Jane My mother saw this coming.
Bill (*shaking his head*) I don't need this.
Jane She warned me, but I wouldn't listen. I was young. I was in love. I was invincible.
Bill This will get us nowhere!
Jane I was Head Girl at my school. Can you believe that?

Bill looks away

I had so much talent … Music … Art … Literature. I had it all.
Bill (*moving to her*) You were scared, lonely and unloved. Your mother was so jealous of your talent she had to destroy all your confidence and self-belief.
Jane I had the whole world in my hands. I could have been someone.
Bill You are someone.
Jane Am I?
Bill Yes. You're my wife.
Jane I don't know who got the best deal.
Bill I'm no complaining.

Jane No, you never do. I think that's your worst fault.
Bill No-one ever said marriage was easy.
Jane Not the way we go at it.
Bill Do you regret it?
Jane (*mimicking his accent*) I'm no complaining. (*She turns her back to Bill*)
Bill (*slipping his arms round Jane's waist*) Billy Big Sausage is sorry.
Jane Don't creep. I hate it when you creep.

Bill nibbles Jane's ear

Stop nibbling my ear.

Bill nibbles Jane's ear again

You know I can't be angry when you nibble my ear like that.

Bill does it again

Will you stop it! (*She breaks free*) God, I must be the shallowest woman in England! I'm so pissed off with you and all you have to do is stick your tongue in my ear and I turn into a stupid schoolgirl!
Bill It's just a knack I have. We've got a criminal record now. (*He moves away*)
Jane We?
Bill (*sitting in the chair*) Oh yes. We're married, aren't we? That means we have to share everything.
Jane (*moving to him*) How much did the fine costs come to?
Bill Two hundred pounds.
Jane (*sitting on Bill's lap*) Bloody hell! It wasn't even a decent punch.
Bill It's all right. I'll work some overtime to make it up.
Jane (*looking at Bill*) Bound over for eighteen months … That sounds a bit …
Bill What?
Jane You know …

Bill No, I don't know.

Jane Well, it sounds a bit — kinky.

Bill Does it?

Jane Yeah. When the judge said "bound over", I immediately thought, bondage, whips and nipple clamps!

Bill Put like that, it does sound a bit horny!

Jane See?

Bill But I don't know whether I can stand eighteen months of it!

Jane How about coming upstairs and me getting you bound over for thirty-five minutes?

Bill Going for a personal best are we, mistress?

Jane Only if you're up for it.

Bill Can I appeal?

Jane pulls Bill up by the hand out of the chair

Jane No, but you can throw yourself upon the mercy of the court — for all the good it will do you.

Bill I'm innocent, I tell you!

Jane Yes, but you won't be in the morning.

Bill Oh, if only I could be more masterful in my own house!

Jane (*changing her voice to that of a slave girl*) Tell me what you want sir. (*She walks away*) You know I'd do anything for the master, as long as he don't beat me. (*She stops, with her back to Bill*)

Bill Oh, you're very good; I'll give you that.

Jane Anything you want … (*She turns her head to him*)

Bill Anything?

Jane (*provocatively*) Anything.

Bill (*with a nervous cough*) Well, there is something I'd quite like you to do.

Jane Just ask sir. Nothing is too much or taboo.

Bill Well, I … I — was wondering if you … (*He laughs*) No, no, I couldn't ask you to do that. (*He looks away*)

Jane (*turning Bill's face to her*) I'll do anything your perverted mind desires.

Bill But … But — you're my wife!

Jane (*rubbing her hand up and down his chest*) Not tonight. Tonight you're out of town on a business trip and I'm the whore you've picked up on the firm's expenses. (*She moves him to the chair*)
Bill But I only get luncheon vouchers.
Jane (*pushing Bill back into the chair*) You're spoiling the moment.
Bill Sorry.
Jane (*putting her foot up on the chair*) Just ask me, sir. (*She pulls her dress up, showing her leg*) I could make your wildest fantasies come true tonight. (*She puts his hand on her leg*)
Bill Bloody hell! I can't believe it. I'm too embarrassed to ask!
Jane (*pulling Bill up out of the chair*) Whisper it, sir. Whisper it softly in my ear. For the right price I'll do absolutely anything. Just whisper.

Bill bends forward and whispers in Jane's ear

You can piss off!

Jane pushes Bill back into the chair

I'm not making you a cup of tea!
Bill You said anything!
Jane I'm offering you heavy S and M with whips and all you want is a cup of PG bloody Tips. You really know how to hurt a girl.
Bill I thought that was the idea?
Jane (*grabbing his arm*) I'm going upstairs for a lie down. Are you coming up? (*She pulls his arm*)
Bill In a minute. I just want to watch the local news.

Jane thinks for a moment

Jane Oh God … (*She drops Bill's arm*) I'd die of embarrassment if we were on there! (*She looks in the direction of the TV*)
Bill I didn't see any reporters in the court.
Jane No, well, the County Show's on.
Bill What's that got to do with it?

Jane Thankfully they'd rather watch sheep being dipped than see justice being done.
Bill That's the second time I've had cause to be grateful to sheep.

Jane opens her mouth to speak

Don't ask!
Jane See you in a minute then. (*She kisses him*) Shall I put my lamb's wool jumper on for you?
Bill No, but take up the peg bag.
Jane What for?
Bill Nipple clamps!

Jane thinks about this for a moment, holding her breasts

Jane All right. But seeing's it's our first time, we'll have a rule.
Bill What rule?
Jane Nothing south of the border.
Bill OK, sounds fair. I reckon I've got more to lose there than you.
Jane Right (*She skips to the door*) Don't be long.
Bill I won't.

Jane goes out

Bill sits rounds square in the chair. Something hurts his back. He gets up, takes the cushion off the back of the chair, puts his hands in and pulls out a bottle of gin. He sighs and sits in the chair, looking at the bottle

The Lights cross-fade to the area UC

Bob enters, wheeling on a comfy armchair and carrying his lunch bag and a newspaper. He positions the chair where the old one was, then sits. He drinks tea and reads his paper

Bill enters

Bob Morning, Bill. How's it hanging?
Bill (*rubbing his chest*) Morning Bob. Down and left. (*He notices Bob's chair*)

Bob Your tea's there. (*He points to the second mug and continues reading*)

Bill Right. Ta. (*He picks up his tea and looks at Bob's chair*) That's a fine chair you've acquired for yourself there, Bob. (*He rubs his chest*)

Bob (*looking up*) Yeah, not bad is it? Yours is there. (*He points to the wooden chair then returns the paper*)

Bill is not impressed. He looks at the chair, then rocks it

(*Not looking up*) It's not a wobbly one.

Bill It's not a comfortable one either.

Bob No.

Bill Not like yours.

Bob I wouldn't think so.

Bill Nice chair that.

Bob Not bad.

Bill They'd look even better as a pair. (*He sees he's getting nowhere, so he sits, rubbing his chest*)

Bob (*noticing Bill rubbing*) What's the matter? Got a bit of heartburn have we?

Bill What? … Oh, no. (*He lowers his hand*)

Bob (*putting down his paper*) Come on then, spit it out. I can't pretend I'm not interested any longer. How did it go in court yesterday?

Bill It went as well as can be expected.

Bob I thought I might have to bail you out this morning.

Bill No … No, it was OK.

Bob Come on then, give us the lowdown. How much did they cap you for?

Bill A hundred and fifty pounds, plus costs.

Bob Is that it?

Bill And I was bound over to keep the peace for eighteen months. (*He rubs his chest again*)

Bob God, that will be almost impossible for you.

Bill I'm giving it my undivided attention at the moment.

Bob Well, it could have been worse. What is wrong with your chest? Are you having a heart attack?

Bill What? Oh. (*He stops rubbing*) Bob, what's your opinion on bondage?

Bob Well, I don't know. I've never given it a lot of thought. Not at nine o'clock on a Wednesday morning anyway.

Bill It's just — what with you being a man of such vast sexual experience — I thought you'd probably have a view on it.

Bob (*alert*) Oh, yes, well of course I have.

Bill (*after a pause*) And what is that view?

Bob thinks for a moment

Bob Well, it hurts, don't it?

Bill Ay. (*He rubs his chest*) That's my view as well.

Bob Have you been reading the *Daily Sport* again?

Bill No.

Bob So what did the wife make of it?

Bill She was a bit more keen on it than I was. We started with the pegs then moved on …

Bob thinks for a moment

Bob No, the court case, you plonker!

Bill Oh, she was a wee bit peeved to say the least.

Bob My wife weren't very happy either last night.

Bill She didn't find that number in your pocket, did she?

Bob What number?

Bill You know, the blonde from level five.

Bob No, no, nothing like that. I'm too clever for that, mate. No, it's just we was talking after dinner about things and I said what with all the kids married and gone, I thought it would be a good idea to adopt a little sprog.

Bill (*spitting his tea into his mug*) What? A baby? You want to adopt a baby?

Bob Yeah. Not a real little one – three or four years old, I thought. You know, one that can already walk, talk and don't keep crapping itself.

Bill And what did Mo make of that?

Bob Well, she couldn't see it at first. She thought we was going to have all this free time together. (*He leans towards Bill*) 'Ere, she

only thought we was going to buy a caravan and bugger off
together at weekends, didn't she?

Bill That would be nice.

Bob You are kidding, ain't you? I've got no gypsy blood in me,
mate. Besides, I've got all my other ladies to consider. How can
I be shagging them when I'm sat in a poxy caravan on the Isle of
Wight? As gifted as I am, mate, there is a limit.

Bill But adopting a baby? It's a huge step.

Bob Oh yeah.

Bill You've never mentioned it before.

Bob No, well, I'm a very deep man, Bill. I keep a lot inside.

Bill Just a pity you can't keep Percy inside your pants, really!

Bob thinks for a moment

Bob Yeah. You haven't got any kids, have you, Bill?

Bill No! And if I did, I wouldn't let you have one.

Bob No, I mean you and Jane. You've never had any kids?

Bill (*after a pause*) We did have a little girl once, but she died.

Bob (*shocked*) I'm sorry, Bill. I didn't realize.

Bill It's all right. It was some time ago. (*Pause*) Cot death. She was
only ten months old.

Bob Bloody hell. I'm sorry, mate.

Bill Ay, well. These things happen. (*Pause*) She'd be coming up
four now.

Bob (*standing, not knowing what else to do*) Here, have my chair.

Bill No, I'm fine.

Bob Go on. Try her out.

Bill Are you sure?

Bob Of course. Feel free.

Bill Thanks. (*He sits in Bob's chair*)

Bob sits on Bill's chair but can't get comfortable

Oh, yes. This is the business.

Bob (*quickly*) It's only for today, mind. Don't go getting any ideas
of grandeur. (*He searches his bag and gets out an envelope*) Here.
I've got something for you. (*He holds the envelope out to Bill*)

Bill (*warily*) What is it?
Bob Open it and see.
Bill It's not an eviction order from the chair, is it?
Bob Just open it.

Bill takes the letter from Bob, opens and reads it

Bill Oh … That's brilliant. (*Pause*) An invite to your Mandy's wedding reception. (*He slowly puts the letter back in the envelope*) That's very kind of you, Bob.
Bob Mo's really keen to meet you. I've told her all about you and Jane … (*He thinks*) Bloody hell! (*He hits his head with his hand*) I'm so stupid. I never gave it a thought. I'm so sorry, Bill. How could I be so insensitive?
Bill Hey, don't keep trying to walk on eggshells. It's all right.
Bob So, are you coming? Say you will. Mo's parents will be there and they are about as much fun as diarrhoea on a bank holiday.
Bill (*thinking it over*) Well, we'd like to …
Bob Oh, go on. We could have a few beers. The drinks are free 'til nine o'clock.
Bill You're making it awfully tempting but …
Bob What?
Bill Well, we're going to Jane's mum and dad that weekend.
Bob Well, put them off.
Bill I can't … (*Grabbing an excuse from thin air*) He's having a hip replacement.
Bob You're not putting it in, are you?
Bill No, but we promised her mum. You know, moral support and all that?
Bob He never comes to see you when you're legless!
Bill I'm sorry, Bob. We won't be able to make it. (*He hands the invitation back to Bob*)
Bob Well, it's not very often you see a Scotsman refuse anything that's free.
Bill Ay, it goes right against the grain.
Bob Come to think of it, you've never been to any of the firm's Christmas dos either.

Bill No.

Bob Last year, how I never got caught with that redhead from Human Resources, I'll never know. She could do things in a swivel chair that would make a contortionist jealous.

Bill Really?

Bob Mind you, she was good at her job. She certainly knew my best position! (*He laughs*)

Bill Jane and me don't really celebrate Christmas.

Bob Why not? You're not Jewish, are you?

Bill No.

Bob God, what a frightening thought – a Jewish Scotsman! (*He leans over to put the invitation back in his bag*)

Bill Christmas was when …

Bob What?

Bill (*changing his mind*) Well, we've not gone in for it in a big way. (*He picks up Bob's paper and starts to read*)

Bob That's my paper!

Bill Is it? (*He carries on reading*)

Bob Can I at least do the crossword?

Bill removes a page from the paper and gives it to Bob

Thank you, thank you so much! (*He sighs*)

They both look at their parts of the newspaper as the Lights fade

They both exit, Bob carrying the wooden chair

The Lights come up DL *on Bill's front room*

Jane is sleeping in the armchair, holding a three-quarters-empty bottle of gin and with some of her dress buttons undone

Bill enters and sees Jane

Bill Oh no! (*He tries to take the bottle out of her hand*)
Jane (*still half asleep*) No! (*She pushes his hand away*)

Bill Please Jane, there's a good girl. Let me have the bottle.
Jane No, Laura. No, Mummy needs it, it's her medicine. But shhhhhhhh — our secret ... Don't tell Daddy.
Bill Daddy already knows. (*He pulls the bottle from her hand*)
Jane (*jumping awake; shouting*) Laura! (*She looks around wildly*)
Bill No, it's me.

Jane composes herself, sits back in the chair, sighs and rubs her eyes

Jane What time is it?
Bill Almost two-thirty.
Jane Oh my God!
Bill Where have you been? I've looked all over town for you.
Jane Out.
Bill Where, out?
Jane (*angrily*) I don't know where out. Just out.
Bill Who with?
Jane I haven't got a clue.
Bill How did you get home?

Jane shrugs her shoulders

Why are your buttons undone?
Jane (*looking down*) Ooooops. (*She struggles to do the buttons up*) Don't know.
Bill Who brought you back?
Jane A taxi I think. What is this, a police investigation?
Bill No, that was last month, remember?
Jane Ha ha, very funny.
Bill We haven't got into any trouble again, have we?
Jane We won't know until tomorrow, will we?

Bill sighs

I haven't punched anyone in the chippy again, if that's all you're worried about.
Bill So, who brought you home?

Jane (*angrily*) I don't know! We have this discussion every time I go out.

Bill There wasn't supposed to be any more times!

Jane (*standing; slightly wobbly*) Oh, well, I'm so sorry.

Bill You promised.

Jane Well, I lied, didn't I? God my life is so boring with you. It's little wonder I need a drink!

Bill (*hurt*) I'm going to bed. (*He turns to go*)

Jane (*trying to move after Bill*) No, please! (*She falls over*)

Bill Are you all right?

Jane Please. I'm so sorry. I didn't mean it. I'm a bad wife. I'm sorry. (*She grabs at Bill's jumper from her sitting position*)

Bill It's OK.

Jane You're a good man Billy — and I've let you down again, but I didn't mean to ... I'm a bad wife. (*She sobs*)

Bill (*kneeling and cuddling Jane to him*) Shhhh. No, you're not. You're everything in the world to me.

Jane (*pushing herself away from Bill, sobbing*) I'm a bad wife and I'm a bad mother.

Bill No!

Jane Yes, I am. I lost our baby. I lost our beautiful little Laura!

Bill (*cuddling Jane again*) No, you didn't. It was an accident. You couldn't have prevented it, nobody could.

Jane If I hadn't fallen asleep that night — I could have saved her ... If only I'd stayed awake. (*She pushes herself away again*)

Bill No, you couldn't.

Jane When she needed me most I wasn't there. What sort of mother does that make me?

Bill You were a kind, caring, attentive mother. What happened to our lovely daughter wasn't anybody's fault. Not yours, not mine, nobody's.

Jane All I can remember is holding her that morning and she was so cold — and her little face ... (*She sobs*)

Bill (*cuddling her to him*) Oh, please don't torture yourself like this. Come with me tomorrow. Please, there are people that can help us.

Jane Oh, no. (*She pushes him and crawls towards the table*) You're not getting me to one of those shrinks.

Bill They're not shrinks.

Jane All these years you've tried, but it makes no difference. I've got all the counselling I need right here. (*She holds up the bottle of gin*) Good old Dr Gordon, if you please. He lets me forget, at least until the cold light of morning.

Bill (*grabbing the bottle from her*) That stuff isn't the answer.

They fight over the bottle. Bill succeeds in pulling it away from Jane

Jane How would you know, you pompous pig? You've never touched a drop of drink in your whole life. (*She looks up at him*) And you can stand and preach till hell freezes over, but that bottle you clasp so tightly in your hand is the only comfort God has given me in three years.

Bill But why drink this poison to forget our beautiful little Laura? Remembering her is what helps me come to terms with what happened. She's my rock that helps me get through every day of my life.

Jane For a clever man you can be so stupid sometimes. (*She puts her hand on the bottle*) I don't drink this stuff to forget her. My hope is, I'll pour enough of it down my throat it will help me join her.

Jane pulls the bottle from Bill's hand, at the same time kneeing him in the groin. Bill falls to his knees in agony. Jane slumps in the armchair, takes the top off the bottle and drinks

Bill Dear God! What are we coming to? (*He grabs the bottle, pulling it away from Jane*)

Jane Well, you won't help me. You're more afraid than I am. I don't have the mental strength to end this sham of an existence. And I'm married to a man who's too scared to help me out of it.

Bill You're right. (*He shouts, still in pain*) I am scared!

Jane At least he admits it!!

Bill (*turning to her*) I'm scared of having to live the rest of my life without you.

They look at each other. Pause

Jane You'd be better off without me.
Bill (*kneeling in front of Jane*) No. Never.
Jane (*running her hands over her face*) You're still young — handsome, good teeth. You could be married again within a year to a woman who's not afraid to have your babies.
Bill I don't want anyone else's. You're the women I married — for better or worse.
Jane I'm afraid you've got the worst at the moment.
Bill I'd rather have that than not have you at all.
Jane (*holding Bill's face in her hands*) You really are an incredible man. You let everyone at work think you're a stupid old pisshead, just to take the spotlight away from your gin-soaked wife. If I only ever got one thing right in my whole muddled life, it was the day I walked down the aisle with you. (*She kisses him on the forehead*)
Bill We can get over all of this together. We only need to be strong.
Jane No. (*She stands, pushing past Bill*) You were born strong, it's not so difficult for you. I've had the talent, God knows I've had the talent, but I've never had the staying power. As my dear old mother would say: "You're all dick, my girl, and no balls". (*She thinks*) And no balls.
Bill (*standing; angrily*) The only good thing your mother did in her whole life was to drop dead.
Jane Yes, but she never lost a baby on the way, did she? (*She sits in the chair*) That's the only drawback I can see about joining our daughter — it means my mother is likely to be there.
Bill She'll never be in the same place as you two.
Jane Good. Then you've just talked me into it.
Bill How can you be so selfish? Just what am I supposed to do if you're not here?

Jane beckons him over with her finger. Bill bends to her

Jane You could always join us.
Bill (*shocked*) What? (*He steps back*)

Jane laughs uproariously

What you need is something to glue your life back together,
Jane (*stopping laughing*) Don't ask me ... Please, don't ask me.
Bill What?
Jane You know very well what. You're going to ask me to have another baby.
Bill (*kneeling before Jane*) We need something to stop us falling apart.
Jane You know how I feel about another baby. I would just never be able to trust myself.
Bill That was just bad luck.
Jane And if we had another one, could you absolutely guarantee me it wouldn't happen again?
Bill No, of course ...
Jane (*hard*) No, you couldn't, could you!
Bill All right. (*Pause*) How about adopting one?
Jane What?
Bill If we adopt a baby, two years old or something.

Jane laughs out loud

What's so funny?
Jane You.
Bill Why?
Jane Because you're so naïve. (*She stands, almost falling over Bill*)
Bill I am?
Jane Yes. (*She staggers around Bill*) I've been a drunk for the last three years. I've been fined and bound over for punching a man full in the mouth for being slow with fast food and you think we can just roll up and someone's going to plonk a two-year-old child in my arms and let me look after it? (*She laughs again*) You are precious sometimes. (*She laughs again and steps back to sit on the arm of the chair. She misses and falls down the side of the chair on to the floor*)
Bill Are you all right?

Jane (*staying behind the chair*) I'm OK. Dr Gordon cushioned my fall!

Bill Nothing hurt?

Jane I have damaged something.

Bill What?

Jane (*lifting her head above the chair*) My pride. I think I've pissed my knickers.

Bill Oh God, no.

Jane It's your fault. (*She cries softly*)

Bill Me?

Jane Yes. You made me laugh so much I wet myself!

The Lights cross-fade to the area DR

Mo enters in her wedding outfit. She removes her buttonhole, twists it in her fingers, smiles to herself, then places the buttonhole on the table

There is a noise off

Bob enters. He has his suit on; his tie has slipped down and his top shirt button is undone. He's not drunk, but he's clearly had a drink

Bob (*sitting in a chair*) Well, that's the last one gone. (*He thinks*) All in all, it went quite well, don't you think?

Mo (*glaring at him*) You are joking, aren't you?

Bob Why?

Mo Why did you have to throw that boy out of the reception?

Bob He was drunk.

Mo He was having a good time.

Bob He was annoying people.

Mo He was socializing.

Bob He had too much to say for himself.

Mo He was the Best Man, for God's sake! He's supposed to have a lot to say. (*She sits*)

Bob I've never liked him. I told our Mandy not to have him as Best Man.

Mo It's not really anything to do with Mandy. And it's most definitely not anything you should be poking your nose into.

Bob I was discreet. No-one hardly noticed.

Mo You can't frogmarch the best man off the dance floor and throw him out the fire exit without causing a bit of a scene.

Bob I let him back in when he cooled down, didn't I?

Mo Why do you always have to control everything, Bob?

Bob I don't.

Mo You can't even see it, can you?

Bob See what?

Mo Your own daughter's wedding day and you still had to be the biggest cheese on show.

Bob What's cheese got to do with anything?

Mo Why do you think all three of our girls have got married and left home with the first man that came along?

Bob We were just lucky I guess.

Mo Lucky? They left because you never gave any of them a moment's freedom.

Bob What are you on about now?

Mo You've tried to control all of our lives, from where we went, how long we stopped, who we talked to, even down to what we wore.

Bob You're getting hysterical, woman.

Mo Am I …? Just think about it for a while.

Bob thinks for a moment

Bob I was just being a protective father, as any man would with three daughters.

Mo (*almost sobbing*) You drove them away — all my babies are gone!

Bob Listen to you. You're the one who's overprotective, if anyone is. You and your silly chatter.

Mo I suppose you can't criticize a person for something they just haven't got.

Bob What the hell has brought this on? I've never seen you like this.

Mo (*standing, gathering herself*) You're nothing but a great big bully, Bob.

Bob (*standing and holding the back of his hand to her*) Just shut your gob woman, or so help me …

Mo What you going to do — throw me out? Well, I'll save you the bother. I'm going.

Bob (*uncertainly*) What?

Mo I'm leaving.

Bob Don't be so stupid, woman.

Mo (*turning on Bob*) Don't you call me that … Don't you call me that ever again. Do you hear me?

Bob I didn't mean …

Mo I'm not stupid, Bob. You may have been telling me different for twenty years or more and I might have nearly believed you, but that's all changing now.

Bob This is absurd! (*He turns and walks across the room*)

Mo Is it? (*She moves after him and turns him round*) When have any of my ideas ever been good enough for you? Any of my thoughts ever caused you any concern? Any of my dreams ever been of the slightest interest to you?

Bob But you're my wife.

Mo Yes, well, that may have to change too. (*She turns to the table*)

Bob Mo, you're tired. Things will look better in the morning.

Mo Yes, you're right. I am tired. (*She picks up her buttonhole*)

Bob See.

Mo (*pulling all the petals off the flower; angrily*) I'm tired of having to guard against what I say to you every waking hour. I'm tired of worrying about not having your dinner on the table when you get in from work, or if you'll like it or if it's hot enough or if your favourite shirt's ironed for you to go to the pub in. (*She turns to Bob*) I'm worried sick about being worried. (*She throws the petals all over Bob then sits in the chair*)

Bob stands, gobsmacked, letting the petals fall from him

Bob Listen. (*He moves to place his hand on Mo's shoulder*)

Mo (*turning to him; angrily*) Don't touch me! Don't you *dare* touch me!

Bob (*moving to sit in the other chair, giving Mo a wide berth*) Look, love, we can work this out. If I've been a bit off, I'm sorry, but we can change things. We can make it better.

Mo I'm going away for a few days, Bob.

Bob Where?

Mo It doesn't matter where.

Bob (*getting angry*) Now you look here …

Mo No, you look. If you abuse me now, so help me I'll go for good. (*Pause*) I want to be left alone for a few days to sort things out in my head. (*She looks at Bob*) Push me now Bob, and I'll be gone forever.

Bob (*after a pause*) So come on then — who is it?

Mo (*looking up*) What?

Bob The other man. Who is he?

Mo What other man?

Bob You don't expect me to believe you thought all this up on your own, do you?

Mo Dear God! He doesn't even know he's doing it.

Bob So, who is it?

No answer

Oh, I see. (*He stands*) I've got to guess, have I?

Mo You'd never guess the truth because you've never given me enough credit.

Bob Two can play at that game, my girl.

Mo What game?

Bob If you move out I could get another woman in here just like that. (*He snaps his fingers*)

Mo (*laughing*) Who?

Bob You'd be surprised.

Mo The only woman who'd put up with you is your mother and I doubt she'd do that now.

Bob You'll see. (*Pointing to his chair*) I'll have another woman sat in that seat within a week.

Mo (*shaking her head*) Oh Bob. You really do live in a world of your own, don't you?

Bob (*sitting again*) I bet I've made a right fool of myself at that wedding. Was he there? Was he at the reception?

Mo Do you ever listen to me?

Bob Have you made me a laughing stock in front of my own family and friends?

Mo You've done that yourself, you stupid man.

Bob (*making a fist at her*) Don't you dare call me that!

Mo (*standing; shouting*) No.

There is a long pause

(*Slowly*) It's not very nice, is it?

They stand face to face, then he turns away from her and sits. Pause

Bob (*his voice softer*) I wouldn't blame you if you had someone else.

Mo (*sitting; spelling it out*) There is no other man.

Bob It can't have been a lot of fun for you over the last few years.

Mo It's got nothing to do with that.

Bob It's just as frustrating for me too, you know.

Mo It's never been a problem for me.

Bob (*after a pause*) I don't mind sharing you.

Mo (*looking up*) What?

Bob You're still a young woman. I know you have certain needs, but I still want to be your husband.

Mo (*looking away*) It's not your fault.

Bob I'd take Viagra if the doctor would let me.

Mo What, with your blood pressure?

Bob If it meant keeping you, I'd risk it.

Mo That is not where our problem lies.

Bob I can change, Mo, just give me a chance.

Mo No, you can't. You are what you are.

Bob (*after a pause*) Have I really driven our girls away?

Mo Oh, I don't know.

Bob I'd never be able to live with myself if I thought that.

Mo Maybe we're both to blame. I don't know. I'm going up to the spare room.

Bob (*grabbing her hand*) Mo, please — don't go.

Mo I've got to. For a few days.

Bob Don't say it's for good — please?

Mo I don't know, Bob, and that's the honest truth.

Bob You can't throw away everything we had just like that.

Mo Do you think I'm doing any of this lightly?

Bob (*kissing her hand*) I do love you. Whatever happens, you must believe that. I never meant to take you for granted.

Mo So you say. (*She gives Bob a hard look*)

Bob slowly lets go of Mo's hand. Mo heads out of the room

Bob You have our bed. I'll walk round to our Mandy's house and stay there for the night. I don't like the idea of it being empty for ten days anyway.

Mo (*almost at the door*) OK.

Bob Mo? Do you realize this will be the first night we've not spent together in twenty-two years?

Unable to look at Bob, Mo exits

The Lights cross-fade to the area UC

Bill enters, bringing on a plush swivel chair. He sets it up and sits in it with the back to the audience; he is hunched down so as not to be visible

Bob enters carrying his paper and lunch bag

Bill (*turning in the chair*) Hallo Bob.

Bob Bloody hell. Where did you get that from?

Bill (*patting the side of the chair*) Not bad is it?

Bob Bit flash if you ask me. (*He sits in his chair and reads his paper*)

Bill (*sitting up*) Are you all right, mate?

Bob Yes, why?
Bill You don't seem to be your old self.
Bob No, no, I'm fine.

There is a pause. Bob reads

Bill So how was the wedding then?
Bob All right.

There is a pause. Bob reads

Bill Went off OK then?
Bob Well, if you'd bothered to turn up you'd have known, wouldn't
   you?
Bill Sorry.
Bob (*putting down the paper*) No, I'm sorry, mate. It went well. The
   sun shone all day and she looked a picture.
Bill How's Mo?
Bob (*defensively*) Fine. Why?
Bill Did she enjoy the day?
Bob Of course she did. She's the bride's mother, for God's sake!
Bill (*after a pause*) Where's she gone then?
Bob (*defensively*) Who?
Bill Your Mandy? Where's she gone on honeymoon?
Bob Oh, Barcelona — or somewhere in Italy.

Bill looks at Bob

   Anyway, how was your weekend?
Bill Yeah, all right.
Bob How's your father-in-law's hip?
Bill Oh fine.
Bob Did you manage to get out for a drink at all?
Bill I went the whole weekend without touching a drop, and that
   ain't happened since I was twelve.
Bob Bloody hell. I'm impressed.
Bill (*after a pause*) Bob, what's your opinion on suicide?

Bob puts his paper down and thinks

Bob Well, its dangerous, ain't it?
Bill It's never a real way out of a problem, is it?
Bob What's brought this on?
Bill I just wondered how near the end of your tether you had to be
    to contemplate it?
Bob Well, I'm all right. You needn't worry about me.
Bill You?
Bob I'm in full control of everything thank you.
Bill Except your John Thomas.
Bob (*angrily*) What are you trying to say?
Bill That you can't keep it in your trousers, you dirty old git.
Bob Oh, yeah, right. (*He tries to read*)
Bill Did you sniff anything out at the wedding?
Bob Please, it was my daughter's big day.
Bill That didn't stop you when your last daughter got married.
Bob No, well.
Bill Up against the church hall wall, you said.
Bob Yeah, I know what I said.
Bill With a big finish across the wheelie bin, you said.
Bob It's not something I'm proud of.
Bill You seemed pretty pleased with yourself on the Monday
    morning.
Bob Are you going to let me read this paper or not?
Bill Sorry.

Pause. Bob reads

Still, you'd have to be pretty desperate before it came to that,
wouldn't you?
Bob (*looking up*) What?
Bill Suicide.
Bob For God's sake, that is not going to happen. People have been
    known to survive on their own. (*He gives up trying to read the
    paper. He folds it and puts it on the tea chest*)
Bill (*confused*) Sorry, Bob. I didn't mean to upset you.

Bob I'm not upset. I'm just saying, if push comes to shove, I could quite easily live on my own.

Bill 'Course you could. (*He thinks for a moment*) I don't think I could though. (*He tries to grab the paper*)

Bob pulls it away

Can I have a look at the racing pages, Bob?

Bob Why don't you buy a paper in the mornings?

Bill Why should I when I get to read yours for free?

Bob (*standing*) Here, have my paper. (*He gives Bill the paper and puts his hand in his pocket*) And my hanky. (*He pulls out his handkerchief and puts it on the tea chest; this is is followed by his change and keys*) And my loose change. And the keys to my van. (*He picks up his lunch bag*) And have my bloody sandwiches as well, why don't you? (*He throws the bag on Bill's lap and starts to walk out*)

Bill Bob?

Bob (*stopping*) Yeah?

Bill What you got in the sandwiches?

Bob Bollocks!

Bob storms off

Bill (*shouting after Bob*) Have they got pickle on 'em?

The Lights cross-fade DL *to Bill's front room*

There is a letter pushed into the photo frame

Bill enters

Bill (*shouting*) Jane? Jane? (*He looks around and sees the letter, Slowly, with trembling hands, he picks up the letter, opens it and reads*) Oh, dear God no! (*He sits in the armchair*)

The Lights cross-fade DR *to Bob's kitchen*

Bob stands by the table. A female blow-up doll sits at the table; a large newspaper is propped up in front of the doll so the audience do not know at first to whom Bob is talking

Bob I'm telling you — she'll be sorry. She'll be sorry she ever left this house. I told her … I warned her. I said I'd get someone else in. But would she listen? Would she hell as like. Well now she must pay the price. I saw my mate in the pub last night. (*He puts his hand in his pocket and pulls out a tub of pills*) He got me these. (*He shakes the pills*) Only bloody Viagra, ain't it? (*He looks at the paper*) Are you listening to me? (*He walks angrily to the paper*) Do you understand what this means? I'm ready to put my life on the line for the sake of our relationship and all you can do is sit there with your mouth open. (*He pulls the paper away and we can see who he's talking to. He sits in the other chair, holding his head in his hands*) God help me. I'm talking to polythene Pam.

The Lights cross-fade DL

Bill is still sitting in the chair

Jane enters, slowly walking into the light

Bill slowly lifts his head, not looking at Jane

Jane It appears my mother was right. I am all dick and no balls.
Bill Thank God she was right about something.

Jane takes the letter from Bill and rips it in half

Jane Do you know the number of a good shrink?

Bill jumps up and hugs Jane. Music

The Lights also come up on Bob who sits with his head in his hands. The Lights hold for a while, then slowly fade

CURTAIN

FURNITURE AND PROPERTY LIST

On stage: UC AREA
Two wooden chairs (one wobbly)
Upturned tea chest

DR AREA
Linoleum floor
Table
Two chairs

DL AREA
Carpet
Armchair. Behind cushion: bottle of gin
Small side table. *On it:* photograph in frame

Off stage: Two mugs of tea, lunch bag, newspaper (**Bob**)
Large plate of sausages and mash (**Mo**)
Bottle of sauce (**Mo**)
Glass of water (**Mo**)
Can of beer (**Mo**)
Comfortable armchair, different newspaper (**Bob**)
Three-quarters-empty bottle of gin (**Jane**)
Plush swivel chair (**Bill**)
Third different newspaper (**Bob**)

Personal: **Bob**: bleeper, handkerchief
Mo: leaflet

During lighting change p. 20

Set: In **Bob**'s lunch bag: envelope containing wedding invitation
letter

During lighting change p. 31

Personal: **Mo**: buttonhole

During lighting change p. 36

Personal: **Bob**: change, keys

During lighting change p. 39

Set: Letter in photograph frame in DL area

During lighting change p.40

Set: Blow-up doll with newspaper in DR area

LIGHTING PLOT

Property fittings required: nil
Composite set. Three interiors

To open: UC area lit

Cue 1	**Bob** exits carrying the wobbly chair *Cross-fade to* DR *area*	(Page 8)
Cue 2	**Mo**: "Why do you always shut me out?" *Cross-fade to* DL *area*	(Page 14)
Cue 3	**Bill** sits, looking at the bottle *Cross-fade to area* UC	(Page 20)
Cue 4	**Bill** and **Bob** look at their parts of the newspaper *Fade*	(Page 25)
Cue 5	**Bill** and **Bob** exit *Bring up lights* DL	(Page 25)
Cue 6	**Jane**: "… I wet myself!" *Cross-fade to* DR *area*	(Page 31)
Cue 7	**Mo** looks at **Bob** then walks out *Cross-fade to* UC *area*	(Page 36)
Cue 8	**Bill**: "Have they got pickle on 'em?" *Cross-fade to* DL *area*	(Page 39)
Cue 9	**Bill** sits in the armchair *Cross-fade to* DR *area*	(Page 39)
Cue 10	**Bob**: " … polythene Pam." *Cross-fade to* DL *area*	(Page 40)
Cue 11	**Bill** jumps up and hugs **Jane** *Bring up lights* DR; *hold then slowly fade to black-out*	(Page 40)

EFFECTS PLOT